The S
Somers

The Sayings of

SOMERSET
MAUGHAM

edited by
CECIL HEWETSON

introduction by
FRANCIS KING

DUCKWORTH

First published with new introduction in 1992 by
Gerald Duckworth & Co. Ltd.
48 Hoxton Square, London N1 6PB
Tel: 071 729 5986
Fax: 071 729 0015

Published by arrangement with
the Estate of W. Somerset Maugham
and William Heinemann Ltd.
Introduction and editorial arrangement © 1992 by
Gerald Duckworth & Co. Ltd.

A catalogue record for this book is available
from the British Library

ISBN 0 7156 2440 7

Typeset by Ray Davies
Printed by Redwood Press Ltd, Melksham

Contents

Biographical Note

William Somerset Maugham, the medical student of eighteen, 'ignorant, ingenuous, enthusiastic and callow', was born on 25th January 1874, the youngest of six brothers. His father was solicitor to the British Embassy in Paris, and two of his brothers were also lawyers; one, Frederick, finally became Lord Chancellor, taking the title of Viscount Maugham of Hartfield.

William spent his first ten years in Paris until his father's death in 1884, his mother having died two years before. 'It was France that educated me,' he said, 'France that taught me to value beauty, distinction, wit and good sense, France that taught me to write.'

On leaving Paris he came to live with his father's brother, the Rev. Henry Macdonald Maugham, vicar of All Saints Church in Whitstable. He entered King's School, Canterbury, where Christopher Marlowe, Walter Pater and Hugh Walpole were educated. On leaving school he spent a year in Heidelberg. When he returned home his future was discussed. His uncle was naturally desirous that he should enter the Church, but this he rejected. Other schemes were considered – the Civil

Service, the Law – but eventually it was decided he should be articled to a chartered accountant. After two months he found the work tedious and uncongenial, and he left.

On his own suggestion he proposed to study medicine, and entered St Thomas's Hospital. Here he became a qualified doctor, MRCS and LRCP. In his last year at the hospital he wrote his first novel, *Liza of Lambeth*, drawing largely on his experiences as an obstetric clerk.

After leaving he went to Paris, sharing rooms with Gerald Kelly, later President of the Royal Academy, and meeting Arnold Bennett, George Moore and many other writers and artists.

At the age of forty-six he married Syrie, daughter of Dr Thomas Barnardo. During the First World War he acted as dresser and ambulance driver in a Red Cross Unit in France. Later he joined the Intelligence Department as a secret agent, an experience that formed the basis of his Ashenden stories, recently televised.

At the end of the war he developed tuberculosis and entered the sanatorium of Nordach-on-Dee. Afterwards he travelled widely, and during the next ten years he wrote some of his most successful plays and stories.

During the Second World War he visited the United States on a special good-will mission on behalf of Britain.

After the war he again travelled widely, and returned to France to restore his old home, the Villa Mauresque, which had been used by the Germans as an observation post and almost destroyed. He died in 1965.

His passing may best be expressed in his own words: 'I have fulfilled myself and I am very willing to call it a day.'

Introduction

by Francis King

As a guide to life, Maugham resembled a man who knows every inch of the city in which he was born but who has never ventured out into the surrounding countryside and is fearful of doing so. About the world of getting and spending, of striving and failing, of sexual love and murderous hatred, he knew as much as any writer of his time; but about another, more distant world of spiritual yearnings and satisfactions, he could only surmise. When he did so surmise, as in one of the most popular of all his novels *The Razor's Edge*, the result was unconvincing.

The consequence of this was that, though he certainly had wisdom, that wisdom was a worldly one. 'When people tell you that overtipping creates as much resentment as undertipping, don't you believe them. You can never tip too much,' he told me on one occasion. On another occasion: 'People find it much harder to forgive the good that you do them than the harm.' And on another: 'When you have your back to the wall, it is difficult to see the writing on it.' Such advice was inadequate for eternity but admirable for today.

Like Shaw's, Maugham's most successful creation was his literary persona. He and his narrator resembled each other in being much-travelled, affluent, cynical men of the world; but there the likeness ends. Whereas Ashenden is self-sufficient, detached and contented, Maugham, under the seemingly tranquil exterior, was racked with self-doubt, resentment and guilt. Near the close of his life that exterior, like some japanned surface exposed to a blow torch, began to crack and disintegrate. It was then that he wrote a scandalous attack on his former wife, the interior decorator Syrie Maugham, and attempted to disinherit the daughter he claimed was not his.

Because of the bruising effects of his childhood – his parents were both dead by the time he was ten, he was then brought up by a clergyman uncle whom he hated and despised – and because of his homosexuality, a constant source of shame, it was essential for Maugham that, by becoming extremely famous and extremely rich, he should make himself immune to anything that anyone could do to him or say about him. But behind the defences of fame and money, he remained uncertain and afraid.

This accounts for his extraordinary

touchiness. Guests at Cap Ferrat would make some injudicious remark, commit some social error or go too far in teasing, and a note would later be delivered to their rooms asking them to leave the next morning after breakfast. Such on one occasion was the fate of Raymond Mortimer. Maugham had been bewailing the fact that, with advancing age, he could no longer attract sexual partners. Mortimer then quoted from one of Harry Graham's *Ruthless Rhymes*:

Now when the nights grow long and chilly,
No one wants to poke poor Willy.

So far from being amused, Maugham was furious – 'There is a train which leaves at ten-twenty tomorrow morning. I suggest you catch it.'

This suspicion that people, even those whom he most trusted, might betray him, mock him, do him down, extended to the most trivial contacts. When he arrived in Kobe by ship, I was among those who went aboard to meet him. He would not speak to any of us, after the first greeting, because he suspected that there were errors in his bar-bills: 'I m-m-must just get these b-b-bar b-b-bills right. I've b-b-been charged for things I'm s-s-sure I never had.' Carefully he went through the bills with the barman. Then, that done, he was at last prepared to talk. This was not because of meanness, I am sure, but out of a determination that no one was going to put one over on him.

Unlike his narrator, Ashenden, who so easily falls into conversation with the people destined eventually to become the subjects of his tales, wins their confidence and extracts from them their secrets, Maugham himself was an essentially shy man, who had difficulty both in striking up an acquaintance with anyone to whom he had not been introduced and in being at his ease with anyone not of the same class as his own. It was here that his secretary-companion Gerald Haxton was invaluable to him. On their travels together, it was Haxton who would leave the first-class section of the ship and descend into its bowels, to chat to the less privileged passengers and the crew. When he came across someone who he thought might provide materials for Maugham, he would bring the two together – much as some Egyptian fellaheen might bring to a famous archaeologist a pot which he has dug up. 'Gerald was my eyes and ears,' Maugham once told me. 'He brought me news of the world.' After Haxton's death, his successor Alan Searle performed the same role.

Unlike Wilde and Coward, Maugham was not a witty man. He made amusing remarks, to which his stammer, paradoxically, gave an added sharpness; but they were not the kind of remarks to be remembered and quoted. He was certainly a witty writer. But the wit was not primarily a verbal one. Coward's and Wilde's plays are full of lines so well-known that audiences actually wait for them in gleeful anticipation. No audience ever waited in the same way for a line in *The Circle*. But it is quite as witty as any comedy by Coward, if not by Wilde. The wit is one which arises primarily out of what happens, not out of what is said.

Because, in his self-protectiveness, he could so often be bitchy or rude, many people wrote many unpleasant things about Maugham after his death. But, in all truthfulness, I have little but good to report of him. He was already in his nineties when he arrived in Kyoto, where I was regional director of the British Council. He stayed for a week and during that week I saw him every day, often for hours on end. Such continuous proximity is an excellent test of character. He was extremely frail and tired easily; but never once did he show any anger or even irritability towards me, Alan Searle or anyone else.

Maugham's reputation at that period was far higher in Japan than in England – a fact on which he commented to me, with the sardonic ruefulness of so much of his conversation. 'University professors queue up each morning in my hotel to get me to sign copies of my books. But when I stay in London, no one cares a damn that I'm there.'

Maugham put up some pretence of wishing to be free of the crowds, many of them students, who gathered around him in any temple, garden or museum which we visited; but it was easy to see that all this clamorous attention, as to some pop star, secretly delighted him. On one occasion, he told me how he had taken Johnny Ray, then at the height of his fame as a pop singer, from Cap Ferrat into Toulon. The American fleet was in. 'Not one s-s-sailor recognised m-m-me of course. But they all recognised J-J-Johnny. "J-J-Johnny, J-J- Johnny, J-J-Johnny!" they kept crying out, as they b-b-brandished b-b-bits of paper for him to s-s-sign.'

'How ghastly!'

'G-G-Ghastly? Not at all! Things will really become g-g-ghastly when s-s-sailors stop shouting "J-J-Johnny, J-J-Johnny, J-J-Johnny!" '

Similarly, things would really have become ghastly for Maugham if, with their identifying cries of 'Mom! Mom! Mom!', excited students had ceased to throng around him.

In their reminiscences of Maugham,

people have often written of his
ruthlessness and selfishness. But I myself
saw nothing of this. One evening, at dinner
at my house, Maugham began to look as
though he would at any moment crumble
to dust. The meal over, he told me, in a
voice so faint that I could hardly hear it,
that he must go home. Would I excuse
him? He felt absolutely 'done in'. Of
course, I said; I'd call my Japanese driver
to take him back to his hotel.

He was indignant. 'You can't possibly
ask that boy to drive the car at this hour. I
wouldn't dream of it. Please get a taxi for
me.'

This I then did.

It was I who took Maugham to the Noh
Theatre for the first time. Later he told me
that it had been one of the most
remarkable experiences of his whole life.
Wrinkled and bowed, the great writer had
sat watching while the great actor had
prepared himself for his role: being sewn
into his robes; applying wet white with
infinite care; then taking a hand-mirror
and staring into it for minutes on end, as
though by doing so he could leave his own
body and enter into an alien one.
'Fascinating!' Maugham kept exclaiming
more to himself than to me or Alan Searle.

Was it fanciful of me to think that, in all
this elaborate effortful preparation,
Maugham saw a metaphor of his own

literary career? His original literary talent,
as his early novels all demonstrate, was
slight; but by preparation, as intense,
prolonged and elaborate as that of the Noh
actor, he had solved the secret of how to
enter into another person and so become
him or her. Without that ability, the stories,
each a model of ingenuity, would have
been no more than skilfully constructed
pieces of machinery. It is the total empathy
between author and character that gives
them their fascinating and exhilarating life.

Women

To a woman no man is so desirable as one that a friend is in love with.

A woman wants to feel about her the arms of a man who adores the ground she walks on. She wants to see his face light up when she enters the room. To feel the pleasantly tickling sensation when his arm tremulously steals around her waist.

A woman will always sacrifice herself if you give her the opportunity.

A woman never wants a Paris model so much as when she knows it's just been sold to somebody else.

Luxury saps a woman's nerve, and when she's known it once it becomes a necessity.

A lady on being reproached for burning the candle at both ends: 'Why, I thought that was the very way to make both ends meet.'

In arguing that perfection is not the cause of beauty, Burke asserts that women are very sensible of this; for which reason they learn to lisp, to totter in their walk, to counterfeit weakness and even sickness. Beauty in distress is much the most affecting beauty.

A woman can take philanthropy as a drug to allay the pangs of unrequited love.

I've no doubt that if Cleopatra had been treated with valerian and massage she would never have made such a fool of herself at the Battle of Actium.

A widow is as old as her possible husband, a spinster as young as her latest young man.

No woman is so attractive that she isn't improved by shaded lights and an evening frock.

There's nothing shows a woman off like a good-looking man.

There's something very satisfactory in a well-manicured hand. It gives you a sense of assurance.

No woman can be unhappy if she eats well, sleeps well, dresses well, and she's losing weight.

Women ascribe a great deal of merit to themselves because they are faithful to their husbands. They're naturally faithful creatures and are faithful because they have no particular inclination to be anything else.

There's no reason why a woman shouldn't have a career just as much as a man.

A woman often thinks her career is looking after her husband – running a house for him, entertaining his friends and making him happy and comfortable.

'I don't know what you must think of me' is what most women say to a man when his opinion does not matter two straws to them.

You know, some women can't see a telephone without taking the receiver off and then, when the operator says, 'Number please', they have nothing to say.

Women are funny. When they're tired of a man they tell you so without a moment's hesitation, and if you don't like it you can lump it. But if you're tired of them you're a brute and a beast and boiling oil is too good for you.

A lot of incompetent women talk a great deal of nonsense about housekeeping.

Now that women have broken down the walls of the harem they must take the rough and tumble of the street.

She's too crafty a woman to invent a new lie when an old one will serve.

Unchastity in women ruins their character. They become untruthful and dissipated, lazy, shiftless and dishonest. This is why the experience of ten thousand years has demanded chastity in women.

She's been my greatest friend for fifteen years. I know her through and through, and I tell you that she hasn't got a single redeeming quality.

Everyone knows there is nothing like having a man pay her attention to make a woman look young.

Intuition never fails a woman.

In the well-regulated society of the future women with their executive ability and natural industry will toil from blushing dawn to dewy eve and leave men free to devote themselves to art and literature and the less violent forms of athletics.

A woman can forgive a man for the harm
he does her ... but she can never forgive
him for the sacrifices he makes on her
account.

Cleopatra was forty-eight when Antony
threw away the world for her sake.

Men

A man thinks it quite natural that he
should fall out of love with a woman, but
it never strikes him for a moment that a
woman can do anything so unnatural as to
fall out of love with him.

Men are very funny. Even when they are
in love they are not in love all day long.
They want change and recreation.

If you want men to behave well to you,
you must be beastly to them; if you treat
them decently, they make you suffer for it.

There's nothing men like more than a red
moist mouth.

She's a nice little thing – silly of course, but
that's what men like.

When a man sends flowers it is a sign that
he has admired more women than one.

Men of affluence, whatever their talent,
have seldom brought themselves to take
the pains necessary to produce a solid
body of work.

Man is a gregarious animal. We are members of a herd.

Men are more tolerant of vanity than of conceit; for the vain man is sensitive to our opinion of him and thereby flatters our self-esteem; the conceited man is not and thereby wounds it.

Men are very trivial, foolish creatures. They have kind hearts. But their heads – oh dear, oh dear, it's lamentable, and they are so vain, poor dears.

A man you have known three months always has an advantage over one you have known ten years.

A good dinner and a bottle of champagne have a wonderful effect on the masculine heart.

The fact is, all men have their faults. They are selfish, brutal, and inconsiderate. They are cat-witted.

Men are naturally wicked. I am seldom surprised at anything they do, and never upset.

I am unable to attach any great importance to the philandering of men. I think it's their nature.

Men can't stand boredom as well as women.

Men don't always say what they think – fortunately, or we should always know what they feel.

Men are sweet and good and silly and tiresome and selfish, ingenuous and so simple. You can't help liking them.

Men are so lucky: if they have any character they grow better-looking as they grow older.

Men are weak, and women are so unscrupulous.

Like all weak men he laid an exaggerated stress on not changing one's mind.

Men only abandon their vices when advancing years have made them a burden rather than a pleasure.

You know what men are – when they once get an idea in their heads it's dreadfully difficult for them to get it out again.

Gratitude is often very strong in men so long as it demands from them no particular sacrifice.

Unchastity has no moral effect on men.
They can be perfectly promiscuous and
remain upright, industrious and reliable.

There are only two things that matter to a
normal man. One is money, and the other
is women.

It is in self-sacrifice that man fulfils
himself. It is in giving all he has to those
who are near and dear to him that he
solves the riddle of life and makes out of
his poor little existence a thing of beauty.

Men are always the same. If things go right
they don't notice anything, but if there is
the smallest thing wrong they grumble for
a week.

A man is more likely to be a good man if
he has learned goodness through the love
of God than through a perusal of Herbert
Spencer.

Love & Marriage

Because women can do nothing except love, they've given it a ridiculous importance.

There are some things that two people may know very well, but which it is much more tactful for them to pretend they don't.

Don't you think it's a mistake for husbands and wives to take holidays together? The only reason one takes a holiday is for rest and change and recreation.

It's not the seven deadly virtues that make a man a good husband, but the three hundred pleasing amiabilities.

Few people know how exhausting it is to have a humorist in the family.

Two people must be profoundly indifferent to one another if they never find occasion to disagree.

I have always heard that the National Gallery is a wonderful place for assignations. You never meet any of your friends, and if you do they are there for the same purpose, and pretend not to see you.

Qualities that make a man a good husband: an agreeable temper, a sense of humour and an entire indifference to petty extravagance.

Philandering with a married woman is the most exaggerated form of amusement that has ever been invented.

Men who wear spats always make the best husbands; it means they have neat and orderly minds.

When a woman discovers that her husband has been unfaithful, her male relations invariably try to console her by telling her how shockingly they have treated their own wives.

When a woman says, 'Do you care for me as much as you ever did?', that speech is the rope around love's throat.

It is the simplest thing in the world to have an affair with a woman, but it is a devil of a nuisance to get out of it.

A man wants a wife who can cook his dinner and look after his children.

Promising to love, honour and obey one's husband – the kind of undertaking no one is really expected to carry out.

A wise woman never lets her husband be quite, quite sure of her.

A good wife always pretends not to know the little things her husband wishes to keep hidden from her. That is an elementary rule in matrimonial etiquette.

Women should remember that they have their homes and their name and position and their family, and they should learn to close their eyes when it's possible they may see something they aren't meant to.

All men are born with the knowledge that when they have wounded a woman's soul – and women's souls are easily wounded – the cure is a trifling, but expensive jewel.

Most married couples tell each other far too much.

I can never see why a woman should give up a comfortable home, a considerable part of her income and the advantage of having a man about to do all the tiresome and disagreeable things for her, because he has been unfaithful to her.

What do you mean by the modern wife? A prostitute who does not deliver the goods.

If a man is unfaithful to his wife she is an object of sympathy, whereas if a woman is unfaithful to her husband he is merely an object of ridicule.

Men are naturally polygamous, and sensible women have always made allowances for their occasional lapse.

Women are monogamous. They don't naturally desire more than one man.

Women dislike intelligence in husbands.

Oh, my dear, what a blessed institution marriage is – for women – and what fools they are to meddle with it.

You can't expect a man to go on making love to his wife after three years.

I can tell you I am in love; I can even describe the feelings that my love excites in me; but I cannot communicate my love and feeling to you. If I could I would be in love with the object of my affections, and that might be highly embarrassing to me.

A sensible woman once said: 'Three husbands! That is my ideal. I would live two days a week with each and have Sundays to myself.'

Men don't want to marry. It's not in their nature. You have to give them a little push or you will never bring them to it.

The administration of a certain amount of strychnine and iron could have persuaded Antony that it wasn't worth while to lose an empire for Cleopatra's sake.

People marry from pique, or loneliness, or fear, for money, position, or boredom.

If you think what they call free love is fun you are mistaken. Believe me, it's the most overrated amusement ever invented. It has all the inconveniences of marriage and none of its advantages.

Love is the only real tragedy in life. Death? Well, one expects death. But when one is in love, one never expects love to die.

If a man falls in love with a pretty woman, he falls out of it. But if he falls in love with a plain one, he will be in love with her all his life.

It is woman's nature to be exacting. If she is in love with you it's a nuisance, and a very charming nuisance too.

Would you rather have the placid indifference of nine couples out of ten, or does the cost of a little trouble and a little common sense keep your husband loving you passionately to the end of his days?

Modern love has a very delicate constitution.

Opportunity is the first aid of love.

Matrimonial schemes? Like those of mice and men, they gang oft agley.

There is no greater torture in the world than at the same time to love and to condemn.

One is always rather apt to exaggerate the passion one has inspired other people with.

There is always one who loves and one who lets himself be loved.

We have long passed the Victorian Era when asterisks were followed after a certain interval by a baby.

On Himself

In my strenuous youth, in order to learn
English, I spent part of each day in
copying out certain classical writers whose
style pleased me, reading a little and then
trying to write it from memory.

I can't understand women who complain
they're misunderstood. I don't want to be
understood. I want to be loved.

I do not pretend to be a philosopher, but
merely a man who has throughout his life
been profoundly interested in art.

If I was kept by a woman I'd want to be
kept in style.

I always reserve to myself the privilege of
changing my mind. It's the only one
elderly gentlemen share with pretty
women.

It's not that I want to be a gay dog, but I
want to be a gay dog if I want to.

Often I lie in bed at night and have a good
laugh to myself as I think how quaint life is.

I've always been interested in people, but I've never liked them.

I am either too self-centred, or too diffident, or too reserved, or too shy to be able to be on confidential terms with anyone I know at all well.

I could think of no one among my contemporaries who had achieved so considerable a position on so little talent.

I have a given capacity for seeing my own absurdity, and I find in myself much to excite my ridicule.

I forget who it was that recommended men for their soul's good to do each day two things they disliked ... it is a precept that I have followed scrupulously; for every day I have got up and I have gone to bed.

I have been rated like a schoolboy and abused like a pickpocket. I read that I had neither decorum nor decency and wondered whether the writer would have been so rashly libellous had he known that all my relations were lawyers.

Under a sedate exterior I enjoy high spirits, and I write, as the crickets chirrup, without the anguish of mind some writers confess to.

I own the most delightful habit in the world, the habit of reading, thus providing myself with a refuge from all the distresses of life.

On the Riviera I get sick of this hot sunshine and these garish colours. I want grey skies and a soft rain falling. I want to feel under my feet the grey pavements of an English country town. I want to be able to have a row with the butcher because the steak he sent me yesterday was tough, and I want to browse around second-hand bookshops. I want to be said how-d'you-do to in the streets by people I knew when I was a boy, and I want to have a walled garden at the back of my house and grow roses.

Youth & Age

No one can make yesterday's cold mutton into tomorrow's lamb cutlets.

I suppose it's difficult for the young to realise that one may be old without being a fool.

From the earliest times the old have rubbed it into the young that they are wiser than they, and before the young had discovered what nonsense this was they were old too, and it profited them to carry on the imposture.

When we are young we think we are different from everyone else, but when we grow older we discover we are all very much of a muchness.

One must not judge the sentiments of one generation by those of another.

One's intimate friends are those one makes in one's teens or early twenties.

What makes old age hard to bear is not a failing of one's faculties, mental and physical, but the burden of one's memories.

People are always rather bored with their parents. That's human nature.

It is an illusion that youth is happy, an illusion of those who have lost it; but the young know they are wretched, for they are full of the truthless ideals which have been instilled into them, and each time they come in contact with the real they are bruised and wounded.

The love of parents for their children is the only emotion which is quite disinterested.

Youth is a lovely thing, it has a promptness of fancy, a liveliness, a freshness of outlook, a directness.

Art

Contemplation is a passive state. It does not suggest the thrill, the excitement, the breathlessness, the agitation with which the sight of a beautiful picture, the reading of a beautiful poem, must affect a person of aesthetic sensibility. It is difficult for me to believe that any such person can read certain passages of Shakespeare or Milton, listen to certain pieces by Mozart or Beethoven, see certain pictures by El Greco or Chardin with so tepid a feeling that it can be justly called contemplation.

There are spiritual pleasures as well as physical pleasures, and if we must allow that sexual intercourse, as St Augustine (who knew something about it) declared, is the greatest of physical pleasures, we may admit that aesthetic appreciation is the greatest of spiritual pleasures.

Talent is a mysterious gift of nature for which there is no accounting.

An artist can only develop on the lines which nature has marked out for him. His work of expression is of the essence of his personality and the attempt to assume a new one futile.

The sitter must give something; there must be something in him which excites the painter's sensibility sufficiently to enable him to portray somewhat more than the model's outward seeming. The painter must have a faculty resembling the novelist's by virtue of which he can slip into the skin of the characters he creates and think their thoughts and feel their feelings.

Beautiful serves as a synonym for good or pretty or pleasing or nice or engaging or interesting. Beauty is none of these. It is much more. It is very rare. It is a force. It is an enravishment.

Beauty does not reside in the object. It is the name we give to the specific feeling of pleasure which the object gives us.

Art can give beauty to things which are in nature ugly or displeasing.

The aesthetic sense ... is akin to the sexual instinct, and shares its barbarity.

Certain modern painters might well bear in mind that some things may be so ugly in their representation as to excite disgust.

There is a distinction between the agreeable and the beautiful. The pleasure which the beautiful occasions is independent of all interest. The agreeable is what the senses find pleasing in sensation.

If appreciation of the beautiful is to have any validity, it must depend not on anything so capricious as feeling, but on a mental process.

Our feelings are surely conditioned by our dispositions. So much is this so that I don't think it an exaggeration to say that no two persons see exactly the same picture or read exactly the same poem.

I don't believe the artist who sets to work to create a work of art has any such purpose as aesthetes ascribe to him. If he has, he is didactic or a propagandist, and as such not an artist.

I think it doubtful whether the artist, whatever art he practises, ever achieves the full results he saw in his mind's eye; yet it allays the urge to creation which is at once his delight and his torment.

Whistler asserted that the layman was by his nature a Philistine, and his duty was to accept what the artist oracularly told him.

His only function was to buy the painter's picture in order to provide him with bread and butter; but his appreciation was as impertinent as his censure. That was a farrago of nonsense.

I believe that the artist produces a work of art to exercise his creative fancy, and whether what he creates is beautiful or not is a fortuitous result in which he may well be uninterested. It may be that beauty, like happiness and originality, is more likely to be obtained when it is not deliberately attempted.

The artist's egoism is outrageous; it must be; he is by nature a solipsist and the world exists only for him to exercise upon it his powers of creation.

Art is a mistress who takes more kindly to the lover who chucks her under the chin than to the lover who kisses the hem of her garment.

The painter's claim to be the sole possible judge of painting has anything but its impertinence to recommend it.

A good painter has two chief objects to paint: namely, man and the intention of his soul.

There is nothing so terrible as the pursuit
of art by those who have no talent.

A natural effect can only be got by an
artificial simplicity.

Writing

The English middle class is never without the desire to rise in the social scale, and to have a writer in the family is to the clergyman, the solicitor, the civil servant something of a prestige item.

Women will write novels to while away their pregnancies; bored noblemen, axed officers, retired civil servants fly to the pen as one might fly to the bottle. There is an impression abroad that everyone has it in him to write one book; but if by this is implied a good book the impression is false.

A writer must feel and think, he must read, and he must put himself in the way of gaining experience.

The advice to give a young writer is to write only about the things he knows.

The trouble with our younger authors is that they are all in their sixties.

Casting my mind's eye over the whole of fiction, the only absolutely original creation I can think of is Don Quixote.

America with its mixed population and the multifarious cross-currents of its life, with its vitality, restlessness and adventurous tempo, offers the novelist a far more diverse and inspiring field of action than' our own settled, humdrum and on the whole law-abiding country.

Style must be conditioned by the subject of discourse. A novelist must be colloquial when he reports dialogue, rapid when he narrates action, and restrained or impassioned (according to his idiosyncrasy) when he describes emotion.

It is for the historian, the divine and the essayist to acquire and maintain a settled style.

English is a difficult language to write, and few authors have written consistently with accuracy and distinction. The best way of learning to do this is to study the great masters of the past.

English is a language of harsh consonants, and skill is needed to avoid the juxtaposition of sounds that offend the ear. It is possible by proper placing, the judicious admixture of long words with short, by alternation of consonants and vowels and by alternation of accent, to secure euphony. Of course no one could write at all if he bore these considerations in his conscious mind; the ear does the work.

To write good prose is an affair of good manners. It is, unlike verse, a civil art ... poetry is baroque.

The purpose of imagery is not to divert the reader but to make the meaning clearer to him.

The purpose of simile and metaphor is to impress the meaning on the mind and by engaging the fancy make it more acceptable.

Of late a dreadful epidemic has broken out. Similes are clustered on the pages of our young authors as thickly as pimples on a young man's face, and they are as unsightly. It is detestable to display your cleverness.

I know what happens to a writer of fiction. An idea comes to him, he knows not whence, and so he gives it the rather grand name of inspiration.

How can you write a play of which the ideas are so significant that they will make the critic of *The Times* sit up in his stall and at the same time induce the shop-girl in the gallery to forget the young man who is holding her hand?

It is the middle class that has created the wealth of English literature.

The nobility and gentry, so far as I know, have only produced two poets whose work is definitely a part of English literature, Shelley and Byron, and only one novelist, Fielding.

Why do you trouble about authors? We live in a democratic age. They take the place in society of the fools whom kings kept about their courts in the Middle Ages. They have the advantage that they don't presume on their position to tell one home truths. They're cheap. A dinner and a little flattery is all they want. And they provide their own clothes.

In writing the important thing is less richness of material than richness of personality.

A complicated phraseology which makes it needful to read the sentence a second time to get its meaning is not unwelcome; a profusion of metaphor, giving fancy ample play, a richness of allusion affording you the delight of recognition, are then qualities beyond price.

A character in a writer's head unwritten remains a possession; his thoughts recur to it constantly, and while his imagination gradually enriches it he enjoys the singular pleasure of feeling that there, in his mind, someone is living a varied and tremulous life, obedient to his fancy and yet in a queer wilful way independent of him.

An author is probably the last person who can write fitly of his own work.

I thought to myself: Thank God, I can look at a sunset now without having to think how to describe it. I meant then never to write another book.

Home & Abroad

The Irish, as we know, are inclined to verbosity. With them enough is not as good as a feast.

When someone transplants himself from one country to another he is more likely to assimilate the defects of its inhabitants than their virtues.

The English can never resist getting something for nothing.

One of the things that must strike the sojourner in Spain is the tenderness with which the Spaniards treat children. However tiresome the children are, however intrusive, wilful, noisy, they never seem to lose patience with them.

England is like a woman you're desperately in love with as long as you don't see her, but when you're with her she maddens you so that you can't bear her.

Englishmen are not romantic. It makes them feel absurd.

The French are the only nation who know how to make love. The French are a much more civilised nation than we are and they have come to the conclusion long ago that marriage is an affair of convenience rather than of sentiment.

The Americans, who are the most efficient people on earth … have invented so wide a range of pithy and hackneyed phrases that they can carry on an amusing and animated conversation without giving a moment's reflection to what they are saying and so leave their minds free to consider the more important matters of big business and fornication.

Manners

Not to be sensitive to the interest of his listeners is the first requisite of the good talker.

It's much harder to resist kindness than brute force.

Rudeness is not synonymous with wit.

The right people *are* rude. They can afford to be.

The rapier of irony is more effective as an instrument than the bludgeon of insolence.

False modesty is a sign of ill-breeding.

There are occasions when you want a bull in a china shop.

I hate people who play bridge as though they were at a funeral.

Cheek, push and a gift of the gab will serve very well.

Officiousness is not politeness.

Snobbishness is the spirit of romance in a reach-me-down.

Frankness is often a very effective screen for one's thoughts.

Truth is an excellent thing, but before one tells it one should be quite sure that one does so for the advantage of the person who hears it rather than for one's own self-satisfaction.

I suppose we are meant to be happy, but I don't believe the best way of being that is to try to upset other people's happiness.

People commit murders for reasons that seem good to them, not in order to enjoy a curious experience.

One finds after a time that one can bear the sacrifices that other people make for one.

You mustn't ask from people more than they are capable of giving.

How much less is the sense of obligation in those who receive favours than in those who pay them.

One profits more by the mistakes one makes off one's own bat than by doing the right thing on somebody else's advice.

We learn resignation not by our own suffering, but by the suffering of others.

When I was young and travelled a good deal, I found that the English were detested all over the world because they were so class-conscious and sniffy.

Maxims

There is no such thing as abstract morality.

Organisation means getting someone else to do your job for you if you can and, if you can't, letting it rip.

It's not a very good plan to take other people's misfortunes too much to heart.

Innocence is charming in theory, but in practice experience has many advantages.

Be natural, that's the chief thing. It's the result of infinite pains. It is the final triumph of artifice.

It is so tiresome of our little sins to look foolish when they are found out, instead of wicked.

Hypocrisy is the most difficult and nerve-racking vice that any man can pursue; it needs an unceasing vigilance and a rare detachment of spirit. It cannot, like adultery or gluttony, be practised at spare moments; it is a whole-time job.

Good actions are like drug-taking, the first step may lead you heaven knows where.

It's very hard to make friends. It requires that one should give all oneself without a thought of return.

When feeling is the gauge you can snap your fingers at logic, and when your logic is weak that is very agreeable.

Follow your inclinations with due regard to the policeman round the corner.

Guile is the only weapon of the weak against the strong.

Sensual pleasures are the most violent and the most exquisite.

One should always trust one's first impressions.

If one felt about things at night as one does the next morning, life would be a dashed sight easier.

Duty! Stern daughter of the voice of God.

The unfortunate thing about this world is that good habits are so much easier to get out of than bad ones.

Reverence for what somebody said is a stultifying quality: there is a damned sight too much reverence in the world.

It is not very comfortable to have the gift of being amused at one's own absurdity.

Our business is right living. The problem of right living is complicated by the fact that there is no one code for everybody; one's job is to find out what is right for oneself and then follow it.

It's a very good plan to ascribe your own feelings to other people.

One may reasonably ask one thing of life, that it should not tear rents in the illusions it creates.

None of us knows for certain the designs of Providence.

One should always abandon an occupation when it has ceased to be a source of pleasure or profit.

One has to let one's common sense triumph over one's finer feelings sometimes.

It's so stupid to want a thing only when you can't get it.

Pragmatism is the last refuge of those who want to believe the incredible.

The sensual are always sentimental.

The great thing is not to let vanity warp one's reasonable points of view.

Don't let pure humbug obscure your common sense.

There are very few of us who are strong enough to make circumstances.

There is no more lamentable pursuit than a life of pleasure.

It is a great nuisance that knowledge can only be acquired by hard work. It would be fine if we could swallow the powder of profitable information made palatable by the jam of fiction.

You can't learn too soon that the most useful thing about a principle is that it can always be sacrificed to expediency.

One should never go again to a place where one has been happy.

Time sifts the significant from the trivial.

Do you know the most enchanting word in the English language? Perhaps.

When one's made up one's mind to do a thing, it's best to do it at once.

When you have wanted something very badly and it comes at last, it is somehow a little frightening.

There's always something a little melancholy in getting what one wants.

The inevitable is only what a fool has not the wit to avoid.

We are slaves of our past, our circumstances and our surroundings.

Nothing is so pleasant as to think of the sacrifices that one will never have to make.

To be harnessed by the wear and tear of life, and to pass rapidly through it without the possibility of arresting one's course – is not this pitiful indeed? To labour without ceasing, and then, without living to enjoy the fruit, worn out, to depart suddenly, one knows not whither – is not that a just cause for grief?

The philosopher believes not according to evidence, but according to his own temperament; and his thinking merely serves to make reasonable what his instinct regards as true.

It is better to want what you have than to have what you want.

The normal is the rarest thing in the world.

It is cruel to disavow one's mediocrity only when it is too late.

What do the circumstances of life matter if your dreams make you lord paramount of time and place?

It's asking a great deal that things should appeal to your reason as well as to your sense of the aesthetic.

The inward life might be as manifold, as varied, as rich with experience, as the life of one who conquered realms and explored unknown lands.

It is not true that suffering ennobles the character; happiness does that sometimes, but suffering, for the most part, makes men petty and vindictive.

The more intelligent a man is, the more he is capable of suffering.

The World

People are never so ready to believe you as when you say things in dispraise of yourself; and you are never so much amazed as when they take you at your word.

In the ordinary affairs of life stupidity is much more tiresome than wickedness.

We all strive for happiness, but what would happiness be if it clung to us like a poor relation?

The best use of culture is to talk nonsense with distinction.

Money is like a sixth sense without which one cannot make a complete use of the other five. The only thing to be careful of is that one does not pay more than twenty shillings for the pound one earns.

People are so unused to the truth that they are apt to mistake it for a joke or a sneer.

The degree of a nation's civilisation is marked by its disregard for the necessities of existence.

Most people have a furious itch to talk about themselves and are restrained only by the disinclination of others to listen. Reserve is an artificial quality that is developed in most of us as the result of innumerable rebuffs.

People do not much like meeting their doctor's wife. They are always afraid she knows too much about their insides.

Everybody is so clever nowadays. They see everything but the obvious.

The only way to be strong is never to surrender to one's weaknesses.

You can do anything in this world if you are prepared to take the consequences, and consequences depend upon character.

If a nation values anything more than its freedom, it will lose its freedom, and the irony of it is that, if it is comfort and money that it values most, it will lose that too.

There is only one freedom: economic freedom.

The whole of life is merely a matter of adding two and two together and getting the right answer.

If you want to be a man you must give up being a gentleman. They have got nothing to do with one another.

Business men do not do things for an ideal.

Do you know that it's harder to get a parlour-maid than a peerage?

It is very unfair to expect a politician to live in private up to the statements he makes in public.

If one wants to be a success in London one must either have looks, wit or a bank balance.

The Army and Navy Stores are a bond of union between all who dwell between the river and St James's Park.

English society is a little pompous; it welcomes a man who can make it laugh.

I don't think you want too much sincerity in society. It would be like an iron girder in a house of cards.

One of the things I've learnt from the war is that a general should choose his own time for a battle.

It is dangerous to let the public behind the scenes. They are easily disillusioned and then they are angry with you, for it was the illusion they loved.

I'll give you my opinion of the human race in a nutshell…. Their heart's in the right place, but their head is a thoroughly inefficient organ.